THE ATOMIC SECRET BY ANCIENT YOGI - THIRUMOOLAR

A LOOK INSIDE THE SMALLEST PARTICLE - ATOM

C POONGAVANAM

ISBN 979-888591433-8

Contents

Foreword

Like some thinkers, I have been involved with nature since childhood. The question of how the universe came into being, the functions of matter, and how the living things came to be, arose in me just like others. If God created the universe, then who created God? Though this question will remain unanswered.

So, nature helped me up with the search for answers very near to my question, and I spent so many days reading many departmental texts. My cognition and energy were clearly in a position to perceive many natural manifestations due to curiosity. Like a lighthouse in the dark, the books improved my knowledge.

The science, history, and spiritual texts that fascinated me led me to it.

With the help of these texts, we were able to gain clarity on the contents of the universe and its functions. Modern science has also provided an opportunity to learn about the atoms responsible for the origin of matter and organisms, as well as many new theories.

At this point, I had to read the Tamil book "Thirumanthiram" by the Indian yogi and philosopher Thirumoolar. Most people do not have knowledge about this book as it is a native Indian book written in Tamil. It is highly unlikely to have been read by even people in India.

The reason it is unpopular is that it was considered a spiritual book and not a scientific one.

But, Thirumanthiram contains ideas about spirituality, the universe, the atom, biology, human physiology, yoga, medicine, etc.

Thus, some of the explanations that Thirumoolar, directly and indirectly, conveys in this book correspond to modern-day scientific functions, ideas about the atom, and some important elements with the numbers of the atom. This is what I will explain in this book.

Most of the ideas expressed in the ancient Vedic texts of India and Tamil texts include information about science, culture, and philosophies of the ancient civilizations which are in line with modern scientific discoveries. In particular, the origin of the universe goes into detail as it includes the five elements of nature and sound, light, atom, and organisms associated with new creation and expansions in the galaxy. New, innovative scientific discoveries occur with the collaborative help of contemporary philosophers, scientists, ultra-modern micro-instruments, giant scientific laboratories, mathematical methods, and computers. But in ancient times physical things were discovered through internal awareness.

None of the scientists agree with some of the current discoveries. In particular, the opinions expressed by scientists are that research results are not always complete. Since then a series of events have taken place, and out of all the discoveries, only some are agreeable.

Moreover, there can be no complete denial in the fundamentals unless there is a difference in their view of such findings. We know that such events continue from ancient times to the present day. Every philosopher, general scientist, and individual must respect and accept the principles, ideas, and discoveries of everyone. Every individual brain has the ability to think differently. Therefore, those who have new zealous thinking, intellectual ability, and research mindset should be accepted by other great scientists. No man can be all-knowing. New policies and inventions can be rolled out to anyone. It depends not only on science but on any field in the world.

If this is the case with contemporary inventions, then how can ancient ideas and inventions be accepted?

But our forefathers, who had the best access to such knowledge, have expressed many scientific ideas directly and indirectly. Ancient knowledge has been explored in theory and practice. Our intelligent ancestors have also found success in their experiments. Modern science continues in the same way through these experiments. I think this book will help cosmologists, science seekers, and researchers alike. Mythological knowledge is thus manifested.

The best scientists are sure to realize this. It is my humble opinion that they should be explored and accepted as it is a research book.

Education I have:

1. Bachelor of Business Administration.

2. Art Master: History.

3. Diploma in Yoga.

4. Divine Will Heals — The Teachings of Paramahamsa Yogananda.

Science courses:

1. Introduction to Astronomy

2. The Growing Universe.

3. Our place in the universe.

4. Astrophysics: Cosmology.

5. Space Success: Space Exploration and Rocket Science.

6. From atoms to stars: How physics describes our world.

7. Cosmic rays, the dark matter and the mysteries of the universe.

8. Origins of the Big Bang and Chemical Components.

9. Astrophysics: Exploring Exoplanets.

10. The best unsolved mysteries of the universe.

11. Earth Hope.

12. One (a) Planet One (a) ocean.

Religious Courses:

1. Religious science.

2. Hinduism through its verses.

General:

1. Public speech.

Thank God for helping me write this book.

My thanks to you too!

Acknowledgements

Texts aided:

Atom science is true wisdom.

Mystery Numbers and the Panchachara Secret.

N. Dhammannachettiyar.

Thirumoolar Thirumanthiram: Explanatory text,

GA.Manikkavasagan.

Autobiography of Paramahamsa Yogananda, A Yogi.

Daily newspaper

Brahma Sutra.

Wikipedia and some websites.

edx website free education,

Science, Vedanta texts, and many other texts.

I would like to thank everyone who helped increase my knowledge.

CHAPTER ONE

The Atomic secret by Thirumoolar:

1.Thirumoolar:

Thirumoolar was a yogi who lived in ancient times. He was also a philosopher. He was endowed with extraordinary powers due to his Thava Yoga practice.

A brief note on the life of Thirumoolar:

Thirumoolar is said to have come from the northern Himalayas of India to Tamil Nadu in southern India. Tamil texts are cited as basic evidence for this. He mastered the art of yoga, which was a great gift to the world from ancient India. As well as being familiar with the oldest scriptures such as the Rig Veda, the Sama Veda, the Atharvanam Veda, and the Yajur Veda. And may have been a connoisseur of many of the arts, spells, and tricks that existed at the time. Ashta (Attama) received the Siddhis.

He reached Thiruvaduthurai, a town inhabited by Tamils in South India, from the Kayalaya hills of northern India. One day when he was passing by, he heard the sound of cows in agony. He went looking for them and found their shepherd lying dead nearby.

Compassionate Thava Yogi Thirumoolar used the rare Attama Siddhi he had learned to move his own soul into the body of the dead shepherd called Moolan. Moolan woke up with the soul of Thirumoolar and the cows were delighted to see this. Thirumoolar then took the cows to their barns safely. When he returned home and saw that Moolan had a wife, he explained to her that Moolan has passed away and Thirumoolar was only using his body when he saw the cows in plight. Moolan's wife doesn't believe Thirumoolar and gathers the village elders to help her. When Thirumoolar explains this to the villagers, they let him go on his way.

When Thirumoolar searches for his own body which he had initially hidden before taking Moolan's body, he found that it had vanished. Hence Thirumoolar realizes that it must be God's work and that the message was to stay in this newfound body. From then he lives in the Moolan's body hence he was called Thirumoolar. After this event, Thirumoolar stayed in Thiruvaduthurai and composed the book Thirumanthiram in 3000 verses.

Ancient Siddharth Thirumoolar's existence period could not be predicted exactly as all his scriptures have been found in varying periods of time dating from as early as before the Common Era 5000 (B.C.E), 3000 (B.C.E), and the Common Era (C.E) from the 5th to the 8th century. This is a testament to the fact that the composition of his songs is similar to that of the Sangakkala in Tamil Nadu, and that some of the lyrics, titles, and lyrics had been considered post-Thiruvalluvar. It can be said that there is no accurate information about the period in which ancient philosophers lived in India, Greece, Rome, and many other countries in general. The possibility of references to later philosophers may have been possible.

But the evidence of the ancients has been destroyed without the maintenance of proper records. Those who do not get the exact period can be identified as ancient philosophers.

Note:

The Sangam period in Tamil Nadu, the southern part of India, was the time around which some of the greatest Kings, Geniuses, and Poets lived and the civilizations thrived under their excellence. The Sangam period refers to the period from the 6th century (BCE) Before the Common Era to the 2nd century (CE) to the present era. During this Sangam period, the best poets in knowledge formed the Sangam and developed the Tamil language. Its period is determined by the Sangam period literature, written by the kings and poets who lived at that time and had given their historical references. They traded with the ancient Roman Empire and the Greek Empire. Through this one can know the antiquity of Tamil Nadu.

• 3 •

CHAPTER TWO

Thirumanthiram Book Composition by Thirumoolar

Ancient Siddharth Thirumoolar composed 3,000 Tamil (verses) songs. This is called Thirumandiram. These are divided into nine Thanthiram hence in Tamil, this is called The Nine Thanthiram.

Thirumanthiram is based on the grammatical practice of the Tamil language in terms of word, meaning, and verse. Then it was compiled into a book. In this book, his ideas are mostly explained clearly about God and the creation of the universe, as well as micro-atoms, human health, biology, human physiology, yoga, spirituality, and many more.

Further,

It also includes Cosmology, Quantum theory, Quantum mechanics, String theory, cosmological sound, light, atmosphere, and biology.

His intellect amazes us. We have created today's modern science based on many modern tools and efficient intellectual thinking based on the ideas given by our ancestors. Through this, many more discoveries have been made and they will continue being discovered in the future. Thirumoolar has made many excellent comments with his superior intelligence. Let us examine only his intellectual prominence.

Before starting, we will try to understand what are atoms, their atomic numbers and elements.

CHAPTER THREE

What is an atom?

Atom refers to the fundamental and smallest particle that makes up an object. Is the smallest particle of an element.

An atom has a positively charged nucleus at its center. Inside the nucleus are protons and neutrons. Neutrons are neutral ones. The nucleus is surrounded by one or more electrons. Each electron has a negative charge. Atoms are the most important structural elements of cosmic matter and organisms; it consists of Atomic light and inherent energy. To this day it remains fully unknown to what extent.

Many texts have to be written to find out what the atom formed in ancient times is. Thus the above explanation of the atom is sufficient for the time being.

What is an element?

An element is a pure substance that cannot be further broken down into separate pieces by physics or chemistry. It is made up of the same type of atoms, not different ones.

Example:

If we take the element gold, it contains only atoms that make up the composition of Gold.

There are 118 elements in total. Of these, 92 elements are present in nature. The remaining 26 elements are synthetically produced in laboratories. Do not assume that the elements exist only outside, in the universe. There are elements in our own physical bodies.

CHAPTER FOUR

What is an atomic number?

The atomic number of an atom is defined as the number of protons present inside the nucleus of that atom or the number of electrons orbiting the nucleus of that element externally.

Each element has a different number of protons and electrons.

The first of these is the hydrogen atom. Its atom is number 1.

The hydrogen atom consists of a proton and an electron. Based on this it is atomic number 1.

Other elements have an atomic number of 2,3,4,5 ..... 118.

The atomic number is denoted by the symbol z.

CHAPTER FIVE

About the atom:

Thirumoolar makes some comments about the atom.

The atom is a microscopic substance that looks like extensive broad hair. The appearance of the Higgs boson (God particle) is like our extensive braided hair. He claims that the atom can split and that it has enormous potential. He also says that the atom will be light and sound and that it can not be destroyed. He says the final form of the atomic split is to be Lord and Uyir (Sivan) (soul). No one says the base of the atom's origin. All of these theories, as stated by Thirumoolar, are in line with those of modern nuclear scientists. No true scientist can deny this. Today scientists are using sophisticated tools to explore the ideas behind the atom. But Thirumoolar knew through his inner awareness.

Therefore, Thirumoolar is an amazing man. The atom has been explored from ancient times to modern times. Ancient Indian and Greek philosophers in particular commented on the atom. There are references to it in many books on the atom from the most ancient times in India. Indian philosophers Ganada (Ganadar) and many more yogis like Thirumoolar have explained the principles of the atom.

Now, let's move on to the research area. Its title is Panchacharam.

CHAPTER SIX

Namasivaya (Panchacharam) – the words of the study:

To know the truth of this word, it is best to speak of its magnificence first.

Panchacharam:

Panchacharam means the five Tamil letters i.e. Namasivaya.

These Namasivaya, the word embodies the forces of the whole universe. As well as due to all the cosmic motions. It is also known as Thiruvaintheluthu(Tamil) by the ancestors.

The word of this Panchacharam (Namasivaya) corresponds to the Tamil numerals.Thirumoolar explains this according to the yogi's words and using the grammatical practices of Tamil.

Tamil Digits:

க - உ - ந - ச - ரூ - சா - எ - அ - கூ - ய - தமிழ் எண்கள் respectively,

In English KA-U-NA-CHA-RU-CHAA-YAE-A-KOO-YA

1- 2- 3 - 4 - 5 - 6 - 7 - 8 - 9 - 10 - Indicates contemporary numbers.

CHAPTER SEVEN

My research results:

I am here, comparing the Tamil numbers mentioned by Thirumoolar and their relation to the present atomic numbers and the elements associated with them.

According to my findings,

I researched whether there was any reason for the ancient Tamil numerals for the word Namasivaya that he said. At the end of that research, I found that the Tamil numbers correspond to the elements with the modern atomic number. Let me inform you that this is my discovery.

The Tamil numerals of the Panchacharam (Namasivaya) correspond to the modern atomic numbers and elements.

Panchacharam | Tamil No. | Modern No. | Atomic No. | Element No.
NA | KA (க) | 1 | 1 | Hydrogen
MA | VU (உ) | 2 | 2 | Helium
CHI | RU (ரு) | 5 | 5 | Boron
VA | YE (எ) | 7 | 7 | Nitrogen
YA | A (அ) | 8 | 8 | Oxygen

You can see how this is in the table above for (நமசிவய)

The word Namasivaya is associated with the atoms of the primordial origin of the universe. There is a consensus among modern scientists that the Universe was created by the Big Bang, and there are differing opinions.

However, according to the Big Bang theory, atoms are formed from where the basic particles appeared. Thus cosmic objects appeared by the fusion of the elements of the first hydrogen and helium atoms. Other substances, such as molecules and compounds, by composite materials, are formed by organisms, so hydrogen and helium are the basic elements. Then other elements are formed. Thus a total of 118 components are formed.

These elements are arranged in a mathematical order, i.e. the first hydrogen atomic number: 1, helium atomic number: 2 and the other elements appear in their atomic numbers 3,4,5,6 ....118 respectively.

This is a natural wonder.

Thus according to the Department of Chemistry,

Chemical elements of the table

Atomic numbers 1 to 118 contains elements.

The elements we have taken here are hydrogen, helium, boron, nitrogen, and oxygen respectively. We are going to know the connection between these and the Panchachara word of Namasivaya.

Therefore, the numbers 1,2,5,7,8 are associated with the Namasivaya characters, let us understand the elements with this atomic number.

CHAPTER EIGHT

NA – KA (க) -1 Atomic Number: 1 Hydrogen & MA –VU (உ) -2 Atomic Number: 2 Helium

The universe expanded and cooled when the Big Bang explosion happened with extreme heat. Thus as the universe cooled many changes took place in space.

In particular basic particles, quarks and electrons were created. Later protons and neutrons were formed. As the temperature of the flame decreased further from 380,000 to 500,000 years after which the electrons were connected by atoms. This gave way to the creation of Hydrogen and helium atoms. Hydrogen is the lightest element and Helium is a noble gas. Hydrogen gas is flammable and explosive. Helium is an inert gas. The first atom of hydrogen formed the second helium atom. This is a very important phenomenon. Hydrogen and helium combine to form clouds, which over time are the result of the galaxies and stars being formed, and the star's nucleosynthesis creates elements and organisms. The vast expansion consists of 73% hydrogen and 25% helium. Its isotopes are the reason for cosmic existence, the sun, and the earth. There is also a vast presence of helium atoms on the surface of the earth.

Hydrogen and helium make up 70% and 28% of the sun, respectively. Hydrogen gas is the primary cause of water formation on Earth. That is, an oxygen atom in a water molecule is bound by two hydrogen atoms, thus creating water. We all know what important role water plays in the formation and existence of living things on earth. Hydrogen is an important factor in the genes of DNA and RNA in the human body. Three of the stars (triple) - due to the alpha process, carbon nuclei combine with extra helium to form a stable isotope of oxygen and energy. It should be noted here that the root cause of everything is Hydrogen.

Helium, for various other reasons, also contributes to the formation of oxygen.

Atoms such as Hydrogen and Helium are therefore important factors in the origin of the universe.

Discovery of Hydrogen and Helium:

The lightest element Hydrogen (gas) was discovered in 1766 by physicist Henry Cavendish. Helium gas was discovered in 1868 by the French astronomer Jules Johnson. While doing this astronomical research in India he saw a yellow line in the solar eclipse spectrum. This is the first evidence for Helium. The chemist Edward Frankland called Helios the cause of this yellow line. Later it was called Helium gas.

CHAPTER NINE

CHI – RU (ㄐㄖ) -5 Atomic Number - 5 Boron

The element Boron is a solid brown substance. It is associated with cosmic rays. Cosmic radiation is a set of nuclear opposite reactions that occur in the universe.

It causes nucleosynthesis, which is formed by the scattering of cosmic rays (cosmic ray gap) for solar objects. It refers to the existence of other chemical elements of cosmic rays on a substance. Boron is an element that promotes the growth of humans, plants, animals, and other organisms. Boron is used to metabolize important vitamins and minerals. (Boric acid). Ribos are biologically formed into a structure with sugar. Traces of boron are found to be essential for the growth of many terrestrial plants. Boron is found in things as basic as a leaf, fruit, tuber, nutty food, milk, which is available through the growth of plants, naturally contributing to the survival of humans and animals. Through foods such as fish and meat, Boron is used in large quantities to sustain life on Earth.

It also plays an important role in bone development, plant growth, drug production, protection from brain degeneration in humans, adenosine (RNA) function, and NAD biological functions, and Boron is thought to be beneficial in the reproductive functions of organisms. It also plays an important role in the concentration of sperm, immunity, and the effective activation of Estradiol.

Boron provides both harmful and beneficial effects on boric acid.

The universe may indirectly help the man with radiation-like contact in a very small percentage.

Modern research reports that scientists believe it may have played a role in the evolution of life on Earth.

The nature of Boron remains a mystery that is not yet fully understood.

Boron Discovery:

Boron was discovered by the French chemists Joseph-Louis, Kay-Lussac and Louis-Jacques Donard, Sir Humphrey Davy in the year 1808.

CHAPTER TEN

VA – YE (எ) –7 Atomic Number –7 Nitrogen

The atmosphere is 78% nitrogen. It is present in about 3% of the human body. Nitrogen in general is a gas that can exist naturally in the universe. It helps in the growth and reproduction of plants and animals. Nitrogen is used to make amino acids in the human body. It makes proteins. Amino acids are the building blocks of all proteins in the human body. Proteins help in the development of structural components in the human body, especially hair, muscles, skin, and tissues, help in metabolism, for the formation of nucleic acids, involved in the inheritance of the atoms of all living things. It helps in the forming of DNA and RNA. DNA contains four nitrogen components, namely adenine, cytosine, guanine, and thymine. Therefore, in the origin of DNA molecules for human evolution, the contribution of Nitrogen is an important factor.

Although Nitrogen is abundant in organic molecules in the environment, it cannot be used by humans directly from air or soil. Humans can get this through natural cycles through microorganisms such as air, soil, water, and green plants.

Therefore the role of Nitrogen is important for the overall growth and existence of the organisms.

Discovery of Nitrogen:

Nitrogen was discovered in 1772 by Daniel Rutherford. He is a Scottish scientist.

CHAPTER ELEVEN

YA - A (அ) - 8 Atomic Number - 8 Oxygen

Oxygen is important for life on earth. All living creatures can only survive by breathing oxygen in some form. Apart from this, there is no other alternative air that can be inhaled for survival. But, plants do photosynthesis. They survive by receiving carbon dioxide from the air and absorbing water from the earth. Oxygen is the third most abundant gas in the universe. At a rate of 21% of the atmosphere, it is approximately 49% by weight of the Earth's surface. In addition, the oceans are 89% Oxygen by weight. Aquatic organisms live by inhaling dissolved oxygen in the water. Oxygen reacts with most components and compounds.

Oxygen gas is responsible for all the functions of molecules for the development of their structural components such as proteins, carbohydrates, and fats in humans and other organisms. Hydrogen and Oxygen (H_2O) are the main cause of water formation. Oxygen, along with other molecules, plays a role in the formation of the DNA molecule. Chemical reactions cause many processes on Earth, such as oxidation, oxygen compression, antioxidant reactions, and photosynthesis. As a result, oxygen reaches a level (with stability) travelling through the Earth's atmosphere. Oxygen is produced in the Earth's atmosphere by the photosynthesis of cyanobacteria that live in water bodies and so do many other organisms living on Earth.

Oxygen Discovery:

In 1774, Joseph Presidly discovered oxygen. He was born in England.

Report on the study of this Namasivaya (Panchacharam) topic

Thirumoolar was a man of extraordinary power. He can be called a sage or a Siddhar or a philosopher. The ideas he conveyed were through inner awareness. Thirumanthiram is a repository of knowledge that teaches many ideas which hide in plain sight. It is excellent research to compare the truths he said with modern scientific ideas. The elements in our body existed before and after the creation of the universe. Similarly, Thirumoolar also states that there is no destruction of cosmic energy.

Moreover, philosophers and yogis were understood to have realized the flow of human thought. So they were able to interpret and communicate what they had learned and felt, indirectly to others. The ancient texts interpreted the philosophies grammatically and considered them to be paradoxical if understood by the unqualified.

Couldn't Thirumoolar have conveyed through his thought the most important elements of the universe?

Realizing these elements he made use of the magical word Namasivaya and called it Panchacharam.

The Tamil numbers for Nama Shivaya are ka-u-ru-ye-a, which corresponds to the modern numbers 1,2,5,7,8.

1,2,5,7,8 refers to the elements in the periodic table with their respective atomic numbers.

I have researched the Tamil numbers he mentioned and the above, in relation to modern atomic numbers. At the end of that research, I found that the Tamil numbers correspond to the modern atomic number elements, which is my discovery.

This is something amazing to all of us.

CHAPTER THIRTEEN

Thirumoolar's view of atomic separation:

Thirumoolar was aware of the nature of the atom. The atomic part is called the very tiny atom (paramaa anu), and then the innermost part of the atom is called a subtle part of the atom consisting of particles like Lepton, Quarks, Gluons, and Higgs Boson.

World Atomic Researchers:

According to the ancient natural scientist Kanada of India, if you separate the matter into smaller pieces and then into even smaller pieces, it becomes indistinguishable at the end. That part, which we arrive at last, is the atom. Atoms are generally in a spherical shape.

He also says that atoms can be bonded by chemical changes caused by other factors such as heat.

Another Siddhar (Tavayogi) from India says that the Thirumoolar atom is a very small object. Claiming that the atom can be divided, he explains the method mathematically.

Other Greek philosophers such as Lucifer and Democritus have also commented on the atom.

Lucifer's Comments:

Materials are all atoms. He says it is indestructible or indistinguishable.

Democritus:

Materials are all made of atoms. It cannot be destroyed or separated. He also says there is space between atoms.

Since the beginning of the 19th century, many scientists in atomic research have developed modern-day nuclear principles through the emergence of new ideas in their thinking. The logic is that any new theory will have reactions approvals and oppositions, but it ultimately leads to new discoveries every day.

This logic led to the development of new approaches, according to new research. New nuclear policies are being redefined as a result of these new approaches. Modern science discovered the origin of the atom, the nature of the atom, its elements, chemical properties, isotopes, its energy, radius, weight, matter, organisms, and its impact on the universe, as well as new atomic theories mostly after the 19th century. Only after this period in history, there was an evolution in many other discoveries based on Atom.

Because of this,

The nucleus of the atom was discovered by Ernest Rutherford, a brilliant physicist from England. Ernest Rutherford was called the father of nuclear physics. He discovered a fact about the most important atom when he carried out the research by injecting alpha particles using modern research equipment. Through this study, he discovered that in the center of the atom there is a nucleus with a very high positive charge in a very small image. He also said that the nucleus of the atom is surrounded and rotated by electrons. He was awarded the 1908 Nobel Prize for his research on the structure of the atom.

The physicist John Dalton published his Atom theory in 1803. He was a native of England who explained modern atomic theory. An atom is a very small particle of matter that is made up of very small, indivisible particles (atoms). He thought that atoms could not be created or destroyed. He explained the elements of the atom and stated its properties as chemical.

Niels Bohr Nuclear Policy:

Niels Bohr is from Denmark, recipient of the 1922 Nobel Prize in Physics. The electron has a negative charge, from which he explains that the electron depends on energy, orbit, and radiation. In a fixed circle, the atom orbits the nucleus in a circular path. Its orbit, i.e.

the path around the electron nucleus, it depends on the size of its orbit, where its energy will vary. He also describes the functions of many atoms.

In addition, there are other Atom researchers namely:

J.J.Thomson, Ernest Rutherford, Max Planck, Ervin Schrodinger, Amedeo Avogadro, R.Stephen Berry, James Chadwick, Marie Curie, Albert Einstein, Frederick Soddy, Otta Hahn.

The list goes on and on, as it is still being explored even today.

Notable among the missing names are the ancient sage Thirumoolar from India. He explains the origin of the atom before modern time and how the atom can be separated. Thirumoolar was also aware of the effects of atoms in the universe.

The atom was first disassembled in 1932 by John Cockraft and Ernest Walton, who learned that modern atomic theories could not separate the atom and that it could later be separated with the help of modern equipment.

Thirumoolar takes an object to get the exact size of the atom and tells us which method can be used to find the atom in that object.

Thus his decisive intellectual and excellent mathematical ability are evident in this method.

According to that method, he explains very clearly the separation of the atom and its size in the following section.

The Seventh Tantra contains a reference song on the atom in 2008, given in Thirumoolar's book Thirumanthiram.

Almighty trying to access the atom inside the atom,

The atomic nucleus inside the atom,

Saying the existence of a thousand more atoms inside an atom,

He who does this has the ability to see the innermost part of the atom.

Subject:

The atom within the atom divides into thousands (fragmented), that part is the primordial causal nucleus.

Research I've done based on what Thirumoolar said:

The nucleus of a helium atom has a nucleus size of 1 femtometer, which when divided by a thousand is the size is the atometer.

Finally according to Thirumoolar, the basic elementary particle of an atom within the atom is called the quarks.

Its size is calculated by,

A very, very small scale of 0.000000000000000001 or $1 * 10^{-18}$.

This microscopic size represents the basic particle called quark.

The volume is calculated by dividing the quark particle inside the atom by a thousand, so the final size is $1e^{-21}$

$1e^{-21}$ stands for 0.000000000000000000001 (Zeptometre).

This is the size that represents the scale of an even more basic particle called Preon.

There are many elementary particles as mentioned above, in the universe. It is from these basic particles that the atom is formed. The atom (elementary particles) is said to be in the form of energy and light, which looks golden to the eyes. Indian philosophers and yogis were the ones who realized the secrets of the atom.

Therefore, atomic light is said to have shape, sound, and immense power. This atomic form is also said to be God. Thirumoolar also approves of this interpretation. The Lord is power and light. The interaction of light atoms can be better understood by understanding this, says Nicola Tesla, the great scientist, who also said that Christ and others knew its secret. This is why many religions consider God to be the light hence importance is placed on the light. All living creatures need light to see. Light might either be in the form of waves or as particles, therefore light and atom stay together.

CHAPTER FOURTEEN

Yogi: Paramahamsa Yogananda explains the following in his autobiography

There are billions of mysteries in the universe, of which light is the most miraculous of these mysteries. Light waves travel everywhere in the universe. According to the theory of wavelengths, light waves propagate between the planets, suggesting that there is an etheric medium called Ether.

Einstein's theory, according to the morphological properties of space, suggests that ether theory can be dismissed as unnecessary. According to any principle, light is the most subtle and independent of any natural object.

The inescapable binary theory of nature has conclusively proven that the source atoms are luminous according to a recently developed electronic magnifier.

The New York Times published a report on the atom at a meeting of the U.S. Council for Scientific Advancement in 1937 about the operation of a sophisticated electronic magnifier.

The inherent properties of the atom are as follows:

The crystal structure of tungsten has not been implicitly known to this day by X-rays. But, now its structure was clearly visible on the photovoltaic screen. In this experiment, Tungsten's 9 atoms appeared in geometric positions among which at the center 1 atom appeared.

On a photovoltaic screen as light, these points are arranged in a geometric pattern on a crystal frame. The molecules in the air that collide against this cube of photons are known as dancing photons, like sunspots glistening in the ripples of water.

The philosophy of electronic magnification was first discovered in 1927 by Dr. Clinton J. Davison and Lester H. German of the Bell Telephone Research Laboratory in New York. As a result of this excellent research, it was found that electronics have the dual properties of a particle and a wave.

Therefore, experiments were carried out on ways to concentrate the electrons in the same way that light rays can be directed through a lens, known as the "Jekyll-Hyde" characteristic of electrons. Dr. Davison was awarded the world's most valuable Nobel Prize in Physics for his outstanding discovery that the whole surface of physical nature is dual in nature.

Einstein proved with his mathematical intelligence that the speed of permanent light in the universe is 186,000 miles (300,000 kilometers). The best scientists with knowledge about Atom say that it is not a material, but it is, as they boldly state energy that is basically the mind, i.e. a source of that nuclear energy.

Moreover, any human being who has realized through inner consciousness that the essence of creation is light can execute the laws of miracles. Whatever form is manifested - be it a tree, a drug, or a human body - the event depends on the yogi's will and his willpower and imagination.

Here an important phenomenon is illustrated. At the beginning of this book, we saw that Thirumoolar's soul passed into the Moolan's dead body. This is what Paramahamsa Yogananda explained above and we understand it is possible for yogi Thirumoolar to use Attama Siddhi to enter the body. This is proof of the incredible feat done by Thirumoolar.

What is Attama siddhi or Asta Siddhi?

Siddhars yoga practice is to finally get miracle energy. Through this practice, the Siddhas gain the ability to control some of the cosmic forces. Also known as the Eight Siddhis. It has extraordinary energy. Powerful yogis in India learned this art. Patanjali, who originated in India, is a great yogi. He is the creator of the philosophy of yoga. This is best explained in the Patanjali's Yoga book.

What are the Attama Siddhis (Eight Siddhis)?

1. Anima: Achieving the transformation of a person's shape into the size of an atom. (Contraction)

2. Mahima: Getting bigger. (Expansion)

3. Iaghima: becoming as weightless as air. (Without weight)

4. Garima: Gaining an immovably heavy nature.

5. Prapti: Appearing any place desirable.

6. Prakamya: Leaving out of one body and moving inside other organisms.

(Flowing from nest to nest)

7. Isitva: Doing what is desired.

8. Vasita: Hypnotizing all, using actions.

As mentioned above are the eight Siddhis.

CHAPTER SIXTEEN

Another mysterious information about light:

There has been interest in aliens from ancient civilizations to the present day. Most of the information about them was light, meaning they came from the sky.

And that those aliens are not bound by the laws of the universe on earth. Those who have met them in person report that objects on Earth have been penetrated by light. As well as claiming that their transportation was light and that its speed was enormous, many countries around the world have evidence about this. Research on this is still going on today.

Why mention aliens here?

Many who have lived on our planet have been found with light (photon) bodies. Evidence for this can be found in ancient texts, inscriptions, and paintings. Yogis were said to have the ability to change the nature of the atom. Therefore Aliens may also have to the same technology or could have acquired the ability to penetrate objects.

So, isn't it possible that Thirumoolar also injected himself into another body like this? This process has already been documented in the past. This can be done by any human, and it could happen again in the future with the proper knowledge and resources. Anything is possible in this universe.

Thus, it is evident that Thirumoolar knew the secret of light and the atom and realized how to use it.

The relationship between light and the atom was explained to illustrate the significance of Thirumoolar and his findings.

I'll explain about two more important concepts:

1. Light.

2. Power.

Today's science makes it very clear that elementary particles have energy and light inside. This is for all the inanimate objects and creatures that are evolving in our universe after the Big bang.

Note:

1. Some of the above explanation is given for understanding only. This may change.

2. The size of a hydrogen atom is 120 picometers.

CHAPTER SEVENTEEN

Thirumoolar explains that life (GOD) is nothing but dividing an object

And in the verse of 2011 given by him in his Thirumandira,

In the wordings of Maeviya Sivan form

Cow's hair is said to be split into one hundred times,

And again if one part of that hundred is split into thousands,

And again one part of that thousand is split into even more hundred thousand times

Then it is God.

Description:

If you take one hair of a cow, split it into a hundred and take one from it, cut it into a thousand, take one out of a thousand and cut it into a lakh part, the amount of hair available indicates the size of the organism.

Mathematically it is explained below:

Cow hair size = 100 microns

100 microns / 0.1 mm

According to Thirumoolar,

Dividing the hair of a cow by one hundred gives its size 0.1 / 100 = 0.001 mm.

Take a section of hair measuring 0.001 mm and divide by 1000,

Divided by 0.001 mm / 1000 mm = 0.000001 mm,

Also, if you take a hair measuring 0.000001 mm and divide it again into 100000 parts,

I.e. 0.000001 mm / 100000 mm = 0.00000000001 mm. Available in sized format.

According to Thirumoolar, the size (figure) of an organism is 0.00000000001 mm or 0.0001 angstroms.

The size of the current hydrogen atom is 0.12 nanometers

Or 1.2 angstrom or 52.900000 picometers, depending on the radius of the van der Waals.

In antiquity, Thirumoolar reported that the smallest life (God) thing was 0.00000000001 mm, which is smaller than a hydrogen atom.

Now the figure of life (GOD) stated by Thirumoolar is 0.0000000000001.

According to this scale, reaches a limit unknown. I.e., Planck Length 6187927353573290100000 Planck Length.

Here time and space are at SINGULARITY.

This amount had very, very subtle energy inside. So, just 13.8 billion years ago, there was a huge explosion caused by this energy.

According to Thirumoolar, the image of life is the Lord. Oneness is symbolized as the divine body. The expression of Thirumoolar's prophetic knowledge is in line with the modern scientific concept

Tamilians were advanced civilizations among other ancient civilizations.

Letters and numbers were used in this civilization ages before other civilizations started using it. Mathematical numbers were used precisely for many scales like:

Tamil Length Dimensions:

10 cone - 1 micro atom

10 micro atoms - 1 atom

8 atoms - 1 small particle (kathir thugal)

8 small particles - 1 thusumpu

8 thusumpu - 1 hair edge

8 hair edge - 1 fine sand

8 fine sand - 1 small mustard

8 small mustard - 1 sesame
8 sesame - 1 paddy
8 paddy - 1 finger
12 fingers - 1 san
2 San - 1 Mulem (18 inches)
4 Mulem- 1 part (72 inches)
6 thousand part - 1 Khatham(12000 yards)
4 Khatham - 1 idea. (48000 yards)

These may have been very precise measurements in ancient times.

Therefore, Thirumoolar has explained in numerical definition how to separate the atom in the ancient times ages before the best physicists of modern times had the intellect, the basic knowledge of the atom, to divide the atom with the help of modern instruments, and to know its microscopic size with the help of modern mathematical methods.

But, Thirumoolar was a prophet who realized how he could use his inner mental energy to split the atom and know its size. His comments on the atom were made in ancient Tamil grammar hence; it was lost to many scholars and researchers. This is an event that should be regretted over time. Traces of pre-existing civilizations in the world are revealed thousands of years later. There are many examples of this. New, innovative discoveries and research are still being made in human history by the works of our ancestors.

One can use Thirumoolar's nuclear principles as an example; it is rare that his nuclear theory would have been available to the people of the world even if it had been discovered.

Moreover, in his book Thirumanthiram there are philosophies necessary for the universe and human society. So, I think this book might help in scientific research today.

It is the duty of true scientists to appreciate the intellectual capacity of the ancient nuclear scientist Thirumoolar. This is the special value we can give him.

Note:

Some scientific ideas may be omitted. The purpose of writing this book is for simple understanding only. The reason is that science is a science that has no limits or end. It is also not appropriate to consider it as a complete scientific text.